50 Hawaiian Recipes for Home

By: Kelly Johnson

Table of Contents

- Hawaiian Poke Bowl
- Lomi Lomi Salmon
- Huli Huli Chicken
- Kalua Pork
- Pineapple Fried Rice
- Haupia (Coconut Milk Pudding)
- Spam Musubi
- Poi (Taro Root Paste)
- Loco Moco
- Teriyaki Beef Skewers
- Guava Glazed Ribs
- Hawaiian Macaroni Salad
- Chicken Long Rice Soup
- Mango Shrimp Ceviche
- Coconut Shrimp
- Haupia Pie
- Sweet and Sour Pineapple Chicken
- Ahi Poke Tacos
- Lau Lau (Pork and Fish Wrapped in Taro Leaves)
- Mai Tai Cocktail
- Pineapple Teriyaki Burgers
- Tuna Poke Nachos
- Grilled Pineapple Salsa
- Hawaiian BBQ Pizza
- Tropical Fruit Salad
- Coconut Prawns
- Taro Bubble Tea
- Pineapple Coconut Smoothie Bowl
- Hawaiian Bread Pudding
- Mango BBQ Chicken
- Tuna Poke Bowl
- Pineapple Upside-Down Cake
- Kalbi Short Ribs
- Hawaiian Acai Bowl
- Coconut Crusted Fish Tacos

- Mango Habanero Chicken Wings
- Hawaiian Sweet Rolls
- Pineapple Coconut Rice
- Hawaiian Seafood Paella
- Macadamia Nut Crusted Mahi Mahi
- Mango Sticky Rice
- Teriyaki Glazed Salmon
- Hawaiian Chicken Katsu
- Pineapple Coleslaw
- Tropical Fruit Popsicles
- Grilled Tofu with Pineapple Salsa
- Hawaiian Lemonade
- Mango Coconut Sorbet
- Hawaiian Sweet Potato Salad
- Coconut Pineapple Bread

Hawaiian Poke Bowl

Ingredients:

For the Poke:

- 1 pound sushi-grade ahi tuna, cubed
- 1/4 cup soy sauce
- 1 tablespoon sesame oil
- 1 tablespoon rice vinegar
- 1 teaspoon grated fresh ginger
- 1 teaspoon honey
- 1 green onion, thinly sliced
- 1 teaspoon sesame seeds
- 1 teaspoon dried seaweed flakes (optional)
- 1 teaspoon Sriracha sauce (optional for heat)

For the Bowl:

- 2 cups cooked white or brown rice, cooled
- 1 cup sliced cucumber
- 1 cup avocado, cubed
- 1 cup mango, cubed
- 1/2 cup radishes, thinly sliced
- 1/4 cup pickled ginger
- 1/4 cup chopped cilantro
- Lime wedges for serving

Instructions:

Prepare the Ahi Tuna:
- In a bowl, combine the soy sauce, sesame oil, rice vinegar, grated ginger, honey, green onion, sesame seeds, dried seaweed flakes, and Sriracha (if using). Mix well to create the poke marinade.

Marinate the Tuna:
- Add the cubed ahi tuna to the marinade, ensuring the tuna is evenly coated. Refrigerate for at least 15-30 minutes to allow the flavors to meld.

Assemble the Poke Bowl:
- In serving bowls, layer the cooked rice as the base.

Arrange Toppings:
- Arrange the marinated ahi tuna, sliced cucumber, avocado cubes, mango cubes, radish slices, pickled ginger, and chopped cilantro on top of the rice.

Garnish:
- Garnish with additional sesame seeds, green onions, and cilantro.

Serve with Lime Wedges:
- Serve the Hawaiian Poke Bowl with lime wedges on the side for an extra burst of flavor.

Enjoy:
- Mix the ingredients in the bowl just before eating to combine the flavors. Enjoy the fresh and vibrant taste of this Hawaiian Poke Bowl, a delightful dish inspired by traditional poke bowls found in Hawaii.

Lomi Lomi Salmon

Ingredients:

- 1 pound fresh salmon fillet, skin removed, diced into small cubes
- 1 cup ripe tomatoes, diced
- 1/2 cup sweet onion, finely chopped
- 1/4 cup green onions, finely chopped
- 1/4 cup cilantro, finely chopped
- 1/4 cup soy sauce
- 2 tablespoons sesame oil
- 1 tablespoon lime juice
- 1 teaspoon fresh ginger, grated
- 1 teaspoon red pepper flakes (optional)
- Salt and black pepper to taste
- Iceberg lettuce leaves for serving

Instructions:

Prepare the Salmon:
- Dice the fresh salmon fillet into small cubes.

Combine Ingredients:
- In a large mixing bowl, combine the diced salmon, tomatoes, sweet onion, green onions, and cilantro.

Prepare the Dressing:
- In a small bowl, whisk together soy sauce, sesame oil, lime juice, grated ginger, red pepper flakes (if using), salt, and black pepper.

Marinate the Salmon:
- Pour the dressing over the salmon mixture. Gently toss to ensure the salmon is well-coated. Refrigerate for at least 15-30 minutes to allow the flavors to meld.

Serve:
- When ready to serve, scoop the Lomi Lomi Salmon onto iceberg lettuce leaves or in a bowl.

Garnish:
- Garnish with additional green onions and cilantro.

Enjoy:

- Enjoy this refreshing and traditional Hawaiian dish that highlights the delicious flavors of fresh salmon and vibrant ingredients. Serve as an appetizer or a light main course.

Huli Huli Chicken

Ingredients:

For the Marinade:

- 4 lbs bone-in, skin-on chicken thighs
- 1 cup pineapple juice
- 1/2 cup soy sauce
- 1/3 cup ketchup
- 1/4 cup brown sugar
- 1/4 cup rice vinegar
- 2 tablespoons ginger, minced
- 2 tablespoons garlic, minced
- 1 teaspoon sesame oil
- 1 teaspoon smoked paprika (optional for smokiness)
- Salt and black pepper to taste

For Basting and Glaze:

- Reserved marinade
- 1/4 cup honey (for glaze)

Instructions:

Prepare the Marinade:
- In a bowl, whisk together pineapple juice, soy sauce, ketchup, brown sugar, rice vinegar, minced ginger, minced garlic, sesame oil, smoked paprika (if using), salt, and black pepper.

Marinate the Chicken:
- Place the chicken thighs in a large resealable plastic bag or a shallow dish. Pour about 3/4 of the marinade over the chicken, reserving the rest for basting. Seal the bag or cover the dish and refrigerate for at least 4 hours or overnight.

Preheat the Grill:
- Preheat your grill to medium-high heat.

Grill the Chicken:

- Remove the chicken from the marinade and let excess drip off. Grill the chicken thighs for about 6-8 minutes per side or until they reach an internal temperature of 165°F (74°C) and have a nice char.

Prepare the Glaze:
- In a small saucepan, heat the reserved marinade over medium heat. Bring it to a boil, then reduce the heat and let it simmer for 5-7 minutes until it thickens slightly. Remove from heat and set aside.

Baste with Glaze:
- During the last few minutes of grilling, baste the chicken with the glaze, turning and basting until the chicken is nicely coated and caramelized.

Check for Doneness:
- Ensure the chicken is fully cooked and juices run clear.

Serve:
- Remove the Huli Huli Chicken from the grill and let it rest for a few minutes. Serve hot.

Enjoy:
- Enjoy this flavorful and sweet-savory Huli Huli Chicken with your favorite sides. It's a classic Hawaiian dish with irresistible tropical flavors.

Kalua Pork

Ingredients:

- 4-5 pounds pork butt or pork shoulder, bone-in or boneless
- 2 tablespoons Hawaiian sea salt or coarse kosher salt
- 2 tablespoons liquid smoke
- Banana leaves or ti leaves (for wrapping - optional)
- 1 cup chicken or vegetable broth (optional, for moisture)

Instructions:

Prepare the Pork:
- Rinse the pork under cold water and pat it dry with paper towels.

Make Incisions:
- Using a sharp knife, make small incisions all over the pork.

Season the Pork:
- Rub the pork generously with the Hawaiian sea salt, making sure to get into the incisions.

Add Liquid Smoke:
- Drizzle the liquid smoke over the pork, rubbing it in with your hands. Ensure the entire surface is coated.

Wrap in Banana Leaves (Optional):
- If you have banana leaves or ti leaves, wrap the pork securely. This step is optional but adds an authentic touch. If not, you can use aluminum foil.

Marinate Overnight:
- Place the seasoned pork in the refrigerator and let it marinate overnight for the flavors to penetrate.

Preheat the Oven:
- Preheat your oven to 325°F (163°C).

Wrap and Roast:
- If not using banana leaves, wrap the pork tightly in aluminum foil. Place it in a roasting pan. Add broth if desired for extra moisture.

Roast the Pork:
- Roast the pork in the preheated oven for about 5-6 hours for a 4-5 pound roast, or until the internal temperature reaches 195-200°F (90-93°C) and the meat is tender and easily pulls apart.

Rest and Shred:

- Allow the Kalua Pork to rest for a few minutes, then shred it using two forks.

Serve:
- Serve the Kalua Pork hot, traditionally accompanied by rice or as part of a Hawaiian plate lunch.

Enjoy:
- Enjoy the smoky, tender, and flavorful Kalua Pork, a classic Hawaiian dish often served during luaus and celebrations.

Pineapple Fried Rice

Ingredients:

- 3 cups cooked jasmine rice, cooled
- 1 cup pineapple, diced
- 1 cup cooked and diced chicken or shrimp (optional)
- 1 cup mixed vegetables (peas, carrots, corn, and/or bell peppers)
- 1/2 cup cashews or peanuts, chopped
- 3 tablespoons soy sauce
- 2 tablespoons fish sauce (optional)
- 1 tablespoon curry powder
- 2 tablespoons vegetable oil
- 3 cloves garlic, minced
- 2 eggs, beaten
- Green onions, chopped (for garnish)
- Fresh cilantro, chopped (for garnish)
- Lime wedges (for serving)

Instructions:

Prep Ingredients:
- Ensure all the ingredients are chopped, diced, and ready to go.

Heat the Wok or Pan:
- Heat vegetable oil in a large wok or skillet over medium-high heat.

Sauté Aromatics:
- Add minced garlic to the hot oil and sauté for about 30 seconds until fragrant.

Add Protein (Optional):
- If using chicken or shrimp, add them to the wok and cook until fully cooked.

Add Vegetables:
- Add mixed vegetables to the wok and stir-fry until they are tender-crisp.

Push Ingredients to the Side:
- Push the ingredients to one side of the wok to make space for the eggs.

Scramble Eggs:
- Pour the beaten eggs into the empty side of the wok. Scramble the eggs until just set.

Combine Ingredients:

- Mix the scrambled eggs with the other ingredients in the wok.

Add Rice:
- Add the cooked and cooled jasmine rice to the wok. Break up any clumps and stir well to combine.

Season with Soy Sauce and Fish Sauce:
- Pour soy sauce and fish sauce over the rice. Add curry powder for flavor. Stir everything together until well combined.

Add Pineapple and Nuts:
- Add diced pineapple and chopped cashews or peanuts to the fried rice. Stir to incorporate.

Taste and Adjust Seasoning:
- Taste the pineapple fried rice and adjust the seasoning if needed, adding more soy sauce or fish sauce according to your preference.

Finish and Garnish:
- Finish by garnishing with chopped green onions and fresh cilantro.

Serve:
- Serve the pineapple fried rice hot, garnished with lime wedges on the side.

Enjoy:
- Enjoy this delicious and colorful Pineapple Fried Rice as a delightful main dish or a side, bringing the tropical flavors of pineapple to your table.

Haupia (Coconut Milk Pudding)

Ingredients:

- 1 cup coconut milk
- 1 cup whole milk
- 1/2 cup sugar
- 1/2 cup cornstarch
- 1/2 cup water
- 1 teaspoon vanilla extract

Instructions:

Mix Cornstarch:
- In a small bowl, dissolve cornstarch in water, ensuring there are no lumps.

Combine Coconut Milk and Whole Milk:
- In a saucepan, combine coconut milk and whole milk over medium heat. Stir in sugar and bring the mixture to a gentle simmer.

Add Cornstarch Mixture:
- Gradually add the cornstarch mixture to the simmering milk, stirring constantly to prevent lumps from forming.

Cook Until Thickened:
- Continue to cook and stir until the mixture thickens to a pudding-like consistency. This usually takes about 5-7 minutes.

Add Vanilla Extract:
- Once the haupia has thickened, remove the saucepan from heat and stir in the vanilla extract.

Pour into Molds:
- Pour the haupia mixture into individual serving molds or a single serving dish.

Cool and Set:
- Allow the haupia to cool at room temperature for a while before transferring it to the refrigerator to set completely. This may take a few hours.

Chill in Refrigerator:
- Let the haupia chill in the refrigerator for at least 2-3 hours, or until it is firm.

Serve:

- Once set, cut the haupia into squares or scoop it out if using a single serving dish.

Garnish (Optional):
- Garnish with toasted coconut flakes or fresh fruit if desired.

Enjoy:
- Serve chilled and enjoy the creamy and coconutty goodness of Haupia, a classic Hawaiian coconut milk pudding often served as a refreshing dessert.

Spam Musubi

Ingredients:

- 2 cups sushi rice, cooked
- 1 can (12 oz) Spam
- 1/4 cup soy sauce
- 1/4 cup oyster sauce
- 1/4 cup sugar
- 5 sheets nori (seaweed)
- Furikake (Japanese rice seasoning, optional)
- Bamboo musubi mold (or plastic wrap and hands for shaping)
- Soy sauce for dipping (optional)

Instructions:

Prepare the Rice:
- Cook sushi rice according to package instructions. Once cooked, let it cool to room temperature.

Slice the Spam:
- Cut the Spam into 1/4-inch thick slices.

Marinate the Spam:
- In a bowl, mix soy sauce, oyster sauce, and sugar. Marinate the Spam slices in this mixture for about 15-20 minutes.

Pan-Fry the Spam:
- In a skillet over medium heat, pan-fry the Spam slices until they are browned and slightly crispy on both sides. Remove from the heat and set aside.

Prepare the Nori:
- Cut each sheet of nori into thirds.

Shape the Musubi:
- Place a sheet of plastic wrap on the musubi mold (or use your hands). Lay a strip of nori on the plastic wrap.

Layer Rice and Spam:
- Wet your hands and place a layer of rice on the nori, pressing it down to form a compact layer. Add a slice of cooked Spam on top of the rice.

Create Layers:

- Add another layer of rice on top of the Spam, pressing down again to make it compact.

Wrap with Nori:
- Fold the nori over the rice and Spam, sealing the edges with a bit of water to help it stick. Press the musubi out of the mold or shape it with your hands.

Repeat:
- Repeat the process until all the Spam slices are used.

Optional Furikake:
- If desired, sprinkle furikake on top of the rice for added flavor.

Slice and Serve:
- Use a sharp knife to cut the musubi into bite-sized pieces.

Serve with Soy Sauce:
- Serve the Spam Musubi with a side of soy sauce for dipping, if desired.

Enjoy:
- Enjoy this popular Hawaiian snack that combines the savory goodness of Spam with the simplicity of sushi rice, all wrapped in a sheet of nori.

Poi (Taro Root Paste)

Ingredients:

- 2 cups taro root, peeled and diced
- Water for boiling
- Salt (optional)

Instructions:

Peel and Dice Taro Root:
- Peel the taro root and cut it into small, evenly sized cubes.

Boil Taro Root:
- Place the diced taro root in a pot and cover with water. Add a pinch of salt if desired. Bring the water to a boil.

Simmer Until Tender:
- Reduce the heat to a simmer and cook the taro until it becomes fork-tender. This typically takes about 15-20 minutes.

Drain and Cool:
- Once the taro is cooked, drain the water and allow the taro to cool for a few minutes.

Mash the Taro:
- Mash the taro root while it is still warm. You can use a fork, potato masher, or a traditional Hawaiian poi pounder.

Adjust Consistency (Optional):
- If the poi is too thick, you can add a little water at a time and continue to mash until you achieve the desired consistency. Traditionally, poi can be thick or thin based on personal preference.

Serve:
- Serve the poi warm or at room temperature.

Enjoy:
- Enjoy this traditional Hawaiian staple either on its own or as a side dish. Poi has a unique texture and flavor that adds a distinctive touch to any meal.

Loco Moco

Ingredients:

For the Burger Patties:

- 1 pound ground beef
- Salt and pepper to taste
- 1 tablespoon Worcestershire sauce
- 1 teaspoon garlic powder (optional)

For the Gravy:

- 2 tablespoons unsalted butter
- 1/4 cup all-purpose flour
- 2 cups beef or chicken broth
- 2 tablespoons soy sauce
- Salt and pepper to taste

For the Eggs:

- 4 large eggs
- Salt and pepper to taste

For Assembly:

- 4 cups cooked white rice
- 4 sunny-side-up fried eggs
- Optional: Chopped green onions for garnish

Instructions:

Prepare Burger Patties:
- In a bowl, combine the ground beef with salt, pepper, Worcestershire sauce, and garlic powder (if using). Form the mixture into four burger patties.

Cook Burger Patties:

- Cook the burger patties on a grill, stovetop, or oven until they reach your desired level of doneness.

Make Gravy:
- In a saucepan, melt butter over medium heat. Add flour and whisk continuously to form a roux. Cook for 1-2 minutes until it turns golden brown.

Add Broth and Soy Sauce:
- Gradually whisk in the beef or chicken broth to avoid lumps. Add soy sauce and continue whisking until the gravy thickens. Season with salt and pepper to taste.

Fry Eggs:
- Fry the eggs sunny-side-up in a separate pan. Season with salt and pepper.

Assemble Loco Moco:
- Place a serving of cooked white rice on each plate. Top the rice with a burger patty, a fried egg, and then generously pour the gravy over the entire dish.

Garnish (Optional):
- Garnish with chopped green onions if desired.

Serve:
- Serve the Loco Moco hot and enjoy the delicious combination of rice, burger patty, fried egg, and savory gravy.

Enjoy:
- Dive into this classic Hawaiian comfort food, known for its satisfying and flavorful combination of ingredients.

Teriyaki Beef Skewers

Ingredients:

For the Teriyaki Marinade:

- 1/2 cup soy sauce
- 1/4 cup mirin (Japanese sweet rice wine)
- 2 tablespoons sake (or dry white wine)
- 2 tablespoons brown sugar
- 2 cloves garlic, minced
- 1 teaspoon ginger, grated
- 1 tablespoon sesame oil (optional, for added flavor)
- 1 1/2 pounds beef sirloin or flank steak, thinly sliced

For Skewers:

- Wooden or metal skewers
- Vegetables of your choice (bell peppers, onions, mushrooms, cherry tomatoes, etc.)

Optional Garnish:

- Sesame seeds
- Chopped green onions

Instructions:

Prepare Marinade:
- In a bowl, whisk together soy sauce, mirin, sake, brown sugar, minced garlic, grated ginger, and sesame oil.

Slice Beef:
- Slice the beef thinly against the grain. This helps in making the beef more tender.

Marinate Beef:
- Place the sliced beef in a resealable plastic bag or shallow dish. Pour half of the teriyaki marinade over the beef, reserving the other half for basting

and serving. Ensure the beef is well-coated. Marinate in the refrigerator for at least 30 minutes to 2 hours.

Preheat Grill or Broiler:
- Preheat your grill or broiler.

Prepare Skewers:
- If using wooden skewers, soak them in water for about 30 minutes to prevent burning. Thread marinated beef slices onto the skewers, alternating with vegetables of your choice.

Grill or Broil:
- Grill the skewers over medium-high heat for about 3-4 minutes per side or until the beef is cooked to your desired doneness. If using a broiler, place the skewers on a broiler pan and broil, turning occasionally.

Baste with Marinade:
- During the last few minutes of cooking, baste the skewers with the reserved teriyaki marinade for extra flavor.

Garnish (Optional):
- Garnish with sesame seeds and chopped green onions, if desired.

Serve:
- Serve the teriyaki beef skewers hot with a side of rice or noodles.

Enjoy:
- Enjoy these flavorful and juicy teriyaki beef skewers as a delicious appetizer or a main course, perfect for a barbecue or a casual dinner.

Guava Glazed Ribs

Ingredients:

For the Ribs:

- 2 racks of baby back ribs
- Salt and black pepper to taste
- 1 tablespoon garlic powder
- 1 tablespoon onion powder
- 1 tablespoon smoked paprika
- 1 teaspoon cayenne pepper (adjust to taste)

For the Guava Glaze:

- 1 cup guava jelly or guava preserves
- 1/4 cup soy sauce
- 2 tablespoons apple cider vinegar
- 2 cloves garlic, minced
- 1 teaspoon ginger, grated
- 1 tablespoon Dijon mustard
- 1 tablespoon honey (optional, for added sweetness)

Instructions:

Prepare the Ribs:
- Remove the membrane from the back of the ribs. Season both sides of the ribs with salt, black pepper, garlic powder, onion powder, smoked paprika, and cayenne pepper. Rub the seasonings into the meat.

Preheat the Oven:
- Preheat your oven to 275°F (135°C).

Wrap Ribs in Foil:
- Wrap each rack of ribs tightly in aluminum foil. Place them on a baking sheet.

Bake:
- Bake the wrapped ribs in the preheated oven for 2.5 to 3 hours or until the meat is tender and easily pulls away from the bone.

Prepare the Guava Glaze:
- In a saucepan, combine guava jelly, soy sauce, apple cider vinegar, minced garlic, grated ginger, Dijon mustard, and honey. Heat over medium heat, stirring until the guava jelly is fully melted and the ingredients are well combined. Simmer for a few minutes until the glaze thickens slightly.

Grill or Broil:
- Preheat your grill or broiler to medium-high heat.

Apply Guava Glaze:
- Carefully unwrap the ribs from the foil. Brush the guava glaze generously over the ribs, coating them on all sides.

Grill or Broil Again:
- Grill or broil the ribs for about 5-10 minutes, turning occasionally and basting with more guava glaze until the ribs develop a caramelized and slightly charred exterior.

Rest and Slice:
- Let the ribs rest for a few minutes before slicing into individual portions.

Serve:
- Serve the guava glazed ribs hot, with any remaining glaze on the side for dipping.

Enjoy:
- Enjoy the sweet and savory goodness of these guava glazed ribs, perfect for a tropical twist on classic barbecue flavors.

Hawaiian Macaroni Salad

Ingredients:

For the Salad:

- 1 pound elbow macaroni
- 1 cup shredded carrots
- 1/2 cup finely diced onion
- 1/2 cup chopped celery

For the Dressing:

- 2 cups mayonnaise
- 1 cup whole milk
- 2 tablespoons apple cider vinegar
- 1 tablespoon sugar
- Salt and pepper to taste

Instructions:

Cook Macaroni:
- Cook the elbow macaroni according to the package instructions. Ensure it's cooked to al dente, and then drain and let it cool to room temperature.

Prepare Vegetables:
- Shred the carrots, finely dice the onion, and chop the celery.

Make Dressing:
- In a bowl, whisk together mayonnaise, whole milk, apple cider vinegar, sugar, salt, and pepper. Adjust the seasoning according to your taste.

Combine Salad Ingredients:
- In a large mixing bowl, combine the cooked and cooled macaroni with shredded carrots, diced onion, and chopped celery.

Add Dressing:
- Pour the dressing over the macaroni and vegetables. Gently toss everything together until well coated.

Chill:

- Cover the bowl with plastic wrap and refrigerate the Hawaiian macaroni salad for at least 2-3 hours, or preferably overnight. Chilling enhances the flavors.

Stir Before Serving:
- Before serving, give the macaroni salad a good stir. If it appears dry, you can add a bit more mayonnaise or milk.

Serve:
- Serve the Hawaiian macaroni salad as a delicious side dish for barbecues, picnics, or any occasion.

Enjoy:
- Enjoy this creamy and slightly sweet Hawaiian macaroni salad that perfectly complements various main dishes.

Chicken Long Rice Soup

Ingredients:

- 1 pound boneless, skinless chicken thighs, thinly sliced
- 8 cups chicken broth
- 1 cup long rice (bean threads or cellophane noodles)
- 1 cup shiitake mushrooms, sliced
- 1 cup bok choy, chopped
- 1 cup carrots, julienned
- 1/2 cup green onions, sliced
- 4 cloves garlic, minced
- 1 tablespoon fresh ginger, grated
- 1/4 cup soy sauce
- 2 tablespoons sesame oil
- Salt and pepper to taste

Instructions:

Prepare Long Rice:
- Soak the long rice (bean threads or cellophane noodles) in warm water until softened. Drain and cut into shorter lengths if desired.

Slice Chicken:
- Thinly slice the boneless, skinless chicken thighs.

Prepare Vegetables:
- Slice shiitake mushrooms, chop bok choy, julienne carrots, mince garlic, grate fresh ginger, and slice green onions.

Cook Chicken:
- In a large pot, heat a bit of oil over medium heat. Add sliced chicken and cook until browned and cooked through. Remove chicken from the pot and set aside.

Sauté Aromatics:
- In the same pot, add a bit more oil if needed. Sauté minced garlic and grated ginger until fragrant.

Add Vegetables:
- Add sliced shiitake mushrooms, chopped bok choy, and julienned carrots to the pot. Cook for a few minutes until the vegetables start to soften.

Pour Chicken Broth:

- Pour in chicken broth and bring the mixture to a simmer.

Add Long Rice:
- Add the soaked and drained long rice to the simmering broth. Let it cook until the long rice is tender.

Return Chicken:
- Return the cooked chicken to the pot.

Season:
- Season the soup with soy sauce, sesame oil, salt, and pepper. Adjust the seasoning according to your taste.

Simmer:
- Let the soup simmer for a few more minutes to allow the flavors to meld.

Add Green Onions:
- Just before serving, add sliced green onions to the soup.

Serve:
- Ladle the Chicken Long Rice Soup into bowls and serve hot.

Enjoy:
- Enjoy this comforting and nourishing soup, filled with tender chicken, flavorful vegetables, and silky long rice.

Mango Shrimp Ceviche

Ingredients:

- 1 pound shrimp, peeled, deveined, and chopped into bite-sized pieces
- 1 cup mango, diced
- 1/2 cup red onion, finely chopped
- 1/2 cup cucumber, diced
- 1/4 cup fresh cilantro, chopped
- 1 jalapeño, finely chopped (seeds removed for less heat, if desired)
- 1 avocado, diced
- 1/2 cup fresh lime juice (about 4-5 limes)
- Salt and pepper to taste
- Tortilla chips for serving

Instructions:

Prepare Shrimp:
- Peel, devein, and chop the shrimp into bite-sized pieces.

Marinate Shrimp:
- In a bowl, combine the chopped shrimp with fresh lime juice. Allow the shrimp to marinate in the lime juice for about 15-20 minutes. The lime juice will "cook" the shrimp.

Combine Ingredients:
- After marinating, add diced mango, finely chopped red onion, diced cucumber, chopped cilantro, and finely chopped jalapeño to the bowl. Mix well.

Add Avocado:
- Gently fold in the diced avocado to avoid mashing it.

Season:
- Season the ceviche with salt and pepper to taste. Adjust the seasoning as needed.

Chill:
- Cover the bowl with plastic wrap and refrigerate the ceviche for at least 30 minutes to allow the flavors to meld.

Serve:
- Serve the mango shrimp ceviche in individual bowls or glasses, garnished with additional cilantro if desired.

Enjoy:
- Enjoy the refreshing and vibrant flavors of this mango shrimp ceviche with tortilla chips for a delightful appetizer or light meal.

Coconut Shrimp

Ingredients:

For the Coconut Shrimp:

- 1 pound large shrimp, peeled and deveined
- 1 cup all-purpose flour
- 1 teaspoon garlic powder
- 1 teaspoon paprika
- 1/2 teaspoon salt
- 1/4 teaspoon black pepper
- 2 large eggs, beaten
- 1 cup shredded coconut
- 1 cup panko breadcrumbs
- Vegetable oil for frying

For the Dipping Sauce:

- 1/2 cup apricot preserves
- 2 tablespoons Dijon mustard
- 1 tablespoon honey
- 1 teaspoon soy sauce

Instructions:

Prepare Shrimp:
- Peel and devein the shrimp, leaving the tails intact if desired.

Set Up Breading Station:
- In separate bowls, prepare three stations for breading: one with flour, garlic powder, paprika, salt, and black pepper; one with beaten eggs; and one with a mixture of shredded coconut and panko breadcrumbs.

Coat Shrimp:
- Coat each shrimp with the flour mixture, then dip into the beaten eggs, and finally, coat with the coconut and breadcrumb mixture, pressing gently to adhere.

Chill Shrimp (Optional):
- Place the breaded shrimp on a baking sheet and refrigerate for about 15-30 minutes. This helps the coating adhere better during frying.

Heat Oil:
- In a large skillet, heat enough vegetable oil over medium-high heat for frying.

Fry Shrimp:
- Fry the coated shrimp in batches for 2-3 minutes per side or until golden brown and the shrimp is cooked through. Don't overcrowd the skillet.

Drain Excess Oil:
- Place the fried shrimp on a paper towel-lined plate to drain any excess oil.

Prepare Dipping Sauce:
- In a small saucepan, heat apricot preserves, Dijon mustard, honey, and soy sauce over low heat, stirring until well combined. Remove from heat.

Serve:
- Serve the coconut shrimp hot with the apricot dipping sauce on the side.

Enjoy:
- Enjoy these crispy and coconutty shrimp as a delightful appetizer or a tasty addition to your meal.

Haupia Pie

Ingredients:

For the Crust:

- 1 1/2 cups graham cracker crumbs
- 1/2 cup unsalted butter, melted
- 1/4 cup granulated sugar

For the Haupia Filling:

- 1 cup granulated sugar
- 1/2 cup cornstarch
- 1/4 teaspoon salt
- 3 cups coconut milk
- 1 cup whole milk
- 1 teaspoon vanilla extract

For the Whipped Topping:

- 2 cups heavy cream
- 1/4 cup powdered sugar
- 1 teaspoon vanilla extract

Optional Garnish:

- Toasted coconut flakes or shredded coconut

Instructions:

Preheat Oven:
- Preheat your oven to 350°F (175°C).

Make Crust:
- In a bowl, combine graham cracker crumbs, melted butter, and sugar. Press the mixture into a 9-inch pie dish, covering the bottom and sides. Bake the crust for about 8-10 minutes or until set. Allow it to cool completely.

Prepare Haupia Filling:

- In a saucepan, whisk together sugar, cornstarch, and salt. Gradually whisk in coconut milk and whole milk until the mixture is smooth. Place the saucepan over medium heat and bring to a simmer, stirring constantly until the mixture thickens.

Cook Haupia Filling:
- Reduce the heat to low and continue cooking for an additional 2-3 minutes, ensuring the mixture is thick and smooth. Remove from heat and stir in vanilla extract.

Pour Filling into Crust:
- Pour the haupia filling into the cooled graham cracker crust. Smooth the top with a spatula and refrigerate for at least 4 hours or until set.

Make Whipped Topping:
- In a chilled bowl, whip the heavy cream, powdered sugar, and vanilla extract until stiff peaks form.

Top the Pie:
- Spread the whipped cream over the chilled haupia filling.

Chill Again:
- Return the pie to the refrigerator and let it chill for an additional 2 hours to set the whipped topping.

Optional Garnish:
- Before serving, you can garnish the pie with toasted coconut flakes or shredded coconut.

Serve:
- Slice and serve this delicious Haupia Pie chilled.

Enjoy:
- Enjoy this tropical Hawaiian treat that combines the creamy coconut goodness of haupia with a buttery graham cracker crust and a fluffy whipped cream topping.

Sweet and Sour Pineapple Chicken

Ingredients:

For the Sweet and Sour Sauce:

- 1 cup pineapple juice
- 1/4 cup ketchup
- 1/4 cup rice vinegar
- 3 tablespoons brown sugar
- 2 tablespoons soy sauce
- 1 tablespoon cornstarch (mixed with 2 tablespoons water to make a slurry)

For the Chicken:

- 1 pound boneless, skinless chicken breasts, cut into bite-sized pieces
- Salt and pepper to taste
- 1/2 cup all-purpose flour
- Vegetable oil for frying

For the Stir-Fry:

- 1 bell pepper, cut into chunks
- 1 onion, cut into chunks
- 1 cup pineapple chunks (fresh or canned)
- 1 tablespoon vegetable oil
- Sesame seeds and chopped green onions for garnish (optional)

Instructions:

Prepare the Sweet and Sour Sauce:
- In a bowl, whisk together pineapple juice, ketchup, rice vinegar, brown sugar, and soy sauce. Set aside. In a small bowl, make a slurry by mixing cornstarch with water.

Coat Chicken:
- Season the chicken pieces with salt and pepper. Coat them in flour, shaking off excess.

Fry Chicken:

- Heat vegetable oil in a skillet or wok over medium-high heat. Fry the coated chicken pieces until golden brown and cooked through. Remove them and set aside on a paper towel-lined plate.

Stir-Fry Vegetables:
- In the same skillet, add a tablespoon of vegetable oil. Stir-fry bell pepper, onion, and pineapple chunks until slightly tender.

Combine Sauce and Finish Dish:
- Pour the prepared sweet and sour sauce into the skillet. Bring it to a simmer. Stir in the cornstarch slurry and cook until the sauce thickens.

Add Chicken:
- Add the fried chicken back to the skillet, tossing to coat it in the sweet and sour sauce. Cook for an additional 2-3 minutes until everything is heated through.

Garnish (Optional):
- Garnish the sweet and sour pineapple chicken with sesame seeds and chopped green onions if desired.

Serve:
- Serve the dish over rice or noodles.

Enjoy:
- Enjoy this delicious and tangy Sweet and Sour Pineapple Chicken as a satisfying meal!

Ahi Poke Tacos

Ingredients:

For the Ahi Poke:

- 1 pound sushi-grade ahi tuna, diced
- 2 tablespoons soy sauce
- 1 tablespoon sesame oil
- 1 tablespoon rice vinegar
- 1 teaspoon honey
- 1 teaspoon ginger, minced
- 1 green onion, thinly sliced
- 1 teaspoon sesame seeds
- 1 avocado, diced

For the Sriracha Mayo:

- 1/4 cup mayonnaise
- 1-2 tablespoons Sriracha sauce (adjust to taste)

For the Tacos:

- Small corn or flour tortillas
- Shredded cabbage or lettuce
- Sliced radishes
- Chopped cilantro
- Lime wedges for serving

Instructions:

Prepare Ahi Poke:
- In a bowl, combine diced ahi tuna with soy sauce, sesame oil, rice vinegar, honey, minced ginger, sliced green onion, and sesame seeds. Gently toss to coat the tuna. Gently fold in diced avocado.

Make Sriracha Mayo:

- In a small bowl, mix mayonnaise with Sriracha sauce. Adjust the amount of Sriracha to your desired level of spiciness.

Assemble Tacos:
- Heat the tortillas in a dry skillet or microwave until warm.

Layer Ingredients:
- Spread a layer of shredded cabbage or lettuce on each tortilla. Spoon a generous portion of ahi poke over the cabbage.

Add Toppings:
- Top with sliced radishes, chopped cilantro, and a drizzle of Sriracha mayo.

Serve:
- Serve the ahi poke tacos with lime wedges on the side.

Enjoy:
- Enjoy these vibrant and flavorful Ahi Poke Tacos as a fresh and delicious seafood taco option!

Lau Lau (Pork and Fish Wrapped in Taro Leaves)

Ingredients:

For the Filling:

- 1 pound pork butt, thinly sliced
- 1 pound fatty fish (such as butterfish or mackerel), deboned and cut into chunks
- 1 cup diced onion
- 1 cup diced tomato
- 1 cup diced green onions
- 1 cup diced carrots
- 1 cup diced sweet potato
- Salt and pepper to taste

For the Taro Leaf Wraps:

- Taro leaves, cleaned and trimmed
- Banana leaves, cleaned and cut into squares
- Kitchen twine or ti leaves (if available) for tying

Instructions:

Prepare Filling:
- In a large bowl, mix together sliced pork, chunks of fish, diced onion, diced tomato, diced green onions, diced carrots, and diced sweet potato. Season with salt and pepper to taste.

Prepare Taro Leaves:
- Clean and trim the taro leaves. If the leaves have thick stems, you can remove them or use a knife to thin them out. Blanch the taro leaves in boiling water for a few seconds to soften them. Pat them dry with a clean kitchen towel.

Assemble Lau Lau:
- Lay out a piece of banana leaf. Place a taro leaf on top of it. Spoon a portion of the filling onto the center of the taro leaf.

Wrap and Tie:

- Fold the taro leaf over the filling to create a bundle. Wrap the banana leaf around the taro leaf bundle. Secure the bundle with kitchen twine or tie it with ti leaves if available.

Repeat:
- Repeat the process until all the filling is used, and you have several lau lau bundles.

Steam or Grill:
- Steam the lau lau bundles for about 3-4 hours until the pork and fish are cooked and tender. Alternatively, you can grill the bundles on a barbecue for a smoky flavor.

Serve:
- Carefully unwrap the banana leaves and taro leaves before serving. Lau lau is traditionally served with rice or poi.

Enjoy:
- Enjoy this Hawaiian delicacy with a unique blend of flavors from pork, fish, and vegetables wrapped in taro leaves!

Mai Tai Cocktail

Ingredients:

- 2 oz white rum
- 1 oz dark rum
- 3/4 oz orange liqueur (such as triple sec or Cointreau)
- 1/2 oz orgeat syrup
- 3/4 oz fresh lime juice
- Pineapple wedge and mint sprig for garnish
- Crushed ice

Instructions:

Prepare Glass:
- Fill a rocks glass with crushed ice.

Shake Ingredients:
- In a cocktail shaker, combine white rum, dark rum, orange liqueur, orgeat syrup, and fresh lime juice. Add ice to the shaker.

Shake Well:
- Shake the ingredients well to chill the mixture.

Strain Into Glass:
- Strain the cocktail into the prepared rocks glass over the crushed ice.

Garnish:
- Garnish the Mai Tai with a pineapple wedge and a sprig of mint.

Serve:
- Serve the Mai Tai immediately and enjoy the tropical flavors.

Optional Float:
- For an added layer of flavor, you can float a small amount of dark rum on top of the finished Mai Tai before garnishing.

Enjoy Responsibly:
- Sip and savor the delicious Mai Tai responsibly, appreciating the balanced blend of rum, citrus, and almond flavors.

Pineapple Teriyaki Burgers

Ingredients:

For the Teriyaki Sauce:

- 1/2 cup soy sauce
- 1/4 cup pineapple juice
- 2 tablespoons brown sugar
- 2 tablespoons mirin or rice vinegar
- 1 tablespoon honey
- 1 teaspoon ginger, minced
- 1 teaspoon garlic, minced
- 1 tablespoon cornstarch (optional for thickening)

For the Burgers:

- 1 1/2 pounds ground beef or a combination of beef and pork
- Salt and pepper to taste
- 4 pineapple rings
- 4 slices Swiss or provolone cheese
- 4 burger buns
- Lettuce, tomato, and red onion for garnish

Instructions:

Prepare Teriyaki Sauce:
- In a small saucepan, combine soy sauce, pineapple juice, brown sugar, mirin or rice vinegar, honey, minced ginger, and minced garlic. Bring the mixture to a simmer over medium heat.

Optional Thickening:
- If you prefer a thicker sauce, mix 1 tablespoon of cornstarch with a little water to make a slurry. Stir it into the sauce and cook until it thickens. Remove from heat.

Season and Shape Patties:
- In a bowl, season the ground meat with salt and pepper. Shape the meat into four burger patties.

Grill Burgers:

- Preheat the grill to medium-high heat. Grill the burgers to your desired doneness, typically 4-5 minutes per side for medium.

Pineapple Rings:
- During the last few minutes of grilling, add the pineapple rings to the grill and cook for about 1-2 minutes per side until they have nice grill marks.

Add Cheese:
- Place a slice of cheese on each burger during the last minute of grilling to allow it to melt.

Assemble Burgers:
- Toast the burger buns on the grill if desired. Place each burger on a bun, top with a grilled pineapple ring, and add lettuce, tomato, and red onion as desired.

Drizzle Teriyaki Sauce:
- Drizzle the prepared teriyaki sauce over the burgers before closing the buns.

Serve:
- Serve the Pineapple Teriyaki Burgers immediately, and enjoy the delicious combination of savory teriyaki flavors with the sweetness of grilled pineapple.

Tuna Poke Nachos

Ingredients:

For the Tuna Poke:

- 1 pound sushi-grade ahi tuna, diced
- 1/4 cup soy sauce
- 1 tablespoon sesame oil
- 1 tablespoon rice vinegar
- 1 teaspoon honey
- 1 teaspoon ginger, minced
- 1 teaspoon sesame seeds
- 2 green onions, thinly sliced
- 1 avocado, diced

For the Nachos:

- Wonton wrappers, cut into triangles and fried (or use store-bought wonton chips)
- 1/2 cup cucumber, diced
- 1/4 cup red onion, finely chopped
- 1/4 cup cilantro, chopped
- 1 jalapeño, thinly sliced
- 1 tablespoon tobiko (flying fish roe), optional
- Lime wedges for serving

For the Sriracha Mayo:

- 1/4 cup mayonnaise
- 1-2 tablespoons Sriracha sauce (adjust to taste)

Instructions:

Prepare Tuna Poke:
- In a bowl, combine diced ahi tuna, soy sauce, sesame oil, rice vinegar, honey, minced ginger, sesame seeds, sliced green onions, and diced avocado. Gently toss to coat the tuna. Set aside.

Make Sriracha Mayo:
- In a small bowl, mix mayonnaise with Sriracha sauce. Adjust the amount of Sriracha to your desired level of spiciness.

Fry Wonton Wrappers:
- Cut wonton wrappers into triangles. Heat oil in a pan and fry the wonton triangles until golden brown and crispy. Alternatively, you can use store-bought wonton chips.

Assemble Nachos:
- Arrange the fried wonton triangles on a serving platter. Spoon the prepared tuna poke over the wonton triangles.

Add Toppings:
- Sprinkle diced cucumber, chopped red onion, cilantro, and thinly sliced jalapeño over the tuna poke.

Drizzle Sriracha Mayo:
- Drizzle Sriracha mayo over the nachos. Optionally, sprinkle tobiko on top for added texture and flavor.

Serve:
- Serve the Tuna Poke Nachos immediately, garnished with lime wedges on the side.

Enjoy:
- Enjoy this fusion of flavors and textures with the freshness of tuna poke on crispy wonton nachos!

Grilled Pineapple Salsa

Ingredients:

- 2 cups fresh pineapple, diced
- 1 red bell pepper, diced
- 1 jalapeño, finely chopped (seeds removed for less heat)
- 1/2 red onion, finely diced
- 1/4 cup fresh cilantro, chopped
- Juice of 1 lime
- Salt and pepper to taste

Instructions:

Preheat Grill:
- Preheat your grill to medium-high heat.

Grill Pineapple:
- Place the diced pineapple on the grill grates and grill for about 2-3 minutes per side or until you see grill marks. The goal is to caramelize the sugars and add a smoky flavor.

Prepare Vegetables:
- While the pineapple is grilling, dice the red bell pepper, finely chop the jalapeño (remove seeds for less heat), and finely dice the red onion.

Chop Cilantro:
- Chop the fresh cilantro.

Combine Ingredients:
- In a bowl, combine the grilled pineapple, diced red bell pepper, chopped jalapeño, diced red onion, and chopped cilantro.

Add Lime Juice:
- Squeeze the juice of one lime over the mixture. Stir well to combine.

Season:
- Season the grilled pineapple salsa with salt and pepper to taste. Adjust the seasoning as needed.

Chill (Optional):
- For enhanced flavors, you can refrigerate the salsa for about 30 minutes before serving.

Serve:
- Serve the Grilled Pineapple Salsa as a refreshing and flavorful topping for grilled meats, fish, tacos, or as a dip with tortilla chips.

Enjoy:
- Enjoy the tropical and smoky goodness of this Grilled Pineapple Salsa!

Hawaiian BBQ Pizza

Ingredients:

For the Pizza:

- 1 pizza dough (store-bought or homemade)
- 1/2 cup barbecue sauce
- 1 1/2 cups shredded cooked chicken
- 1 cup diced pineapple
- 1/2 red onion, thinly sliced
- 1 cup shredded mozzarella cheese
- 1/2 cup shredded cheddar cheese
- Fresh cilantro, chopped, for garnish

For the BBQ Sauce (optional):

- 1/2 cup barbecue sauce
- 2 tablespoons pineapple juice

Instructions:

Preheat Oven:
- Preheat your oven according to the pizza dough package instructions or the recipe if using homemade dough.

Roll Out Dough:
- Roll out the pizza dough on a floured surface to your desired thickness.

Prepare BBQ Sauce (Optional):
- In a small bowl, mix 1/2 cup barbecue sauce with 2 tablespoons of pineapple juice to create a slightly thinned-out barbecue sauce. This step is optional but adds extra flavor.

Assemble Pizza:
- Place the rolled-out dough on a pizza stone or baking sheet. Spread an even layer of barbecue sauce over the dough. Add the shredded cooked chicken, diced pineapple, and thinly sliced red onion. Sprinkle both types of cheese evenly over the top.

Bake:

- Bake the Hawaiian BBQ Pizza in the preheated oven according to the pizza dough package instructions or until the crust is golden and the cheese is melted and bubbly.

Garnish:
- Once out of the oven, drizzle the optional barbecue sauce over the pizza and garnish with chopped fresh cilantro.

Slice and Serve:
- Allow the pizza to cool for a few minutes before slicing. Slice and serve.

Enjoy:
- Enjoy this Hawaiian BBQ Pizza with the sweet and savory combination of barbecue sauce, shredded chicken, pineapple, and red onion!

Tropical Fruit Salad

Ingredients:

- 2 cups pineapple chunks
- 1 cup mango chunks
- 1 cup papaya chunks
- 1 cup kiwi slices
- 1 cup strawberries, hulled and halved
- 1 banana, sliced
- 1/2 cup shredded coconut (optional)
- Fresh mint leaves for garnish

For the Citrus Honey Dressing:

- 1/4 cup orange juice
- 2 tablespoons lime juice
- 1 tablespoon honey
- 1 teaspoon lime zest

Instructions:

Prepare Fruits:
- Cut the pineapple, mango, papaya, kiwi, strawberries, and banana into bite-sized chunks or slices as needed.

Combine in a Bowl:
- In a large mixing bowl, combine all the prepared tropical fruits.

Make Citrus Honey Dressing:
- In a separate small bowl, whisk together the orange juice, lime juice, honey, and lime zest until well combined.

Drizzle Dressing:
- Drizzle the citrus honey dressing over the tropical fruits. Gently toss to coat the fruits evenly in the dressing.

Add Coconut (Optional):
- If using shredded coconut, sprinkle it over the fruit salad and toss gently.

Chill (Optional):
- You can refrigerate the tropical fruit salad for about 30 minutes to allow the flavors to meld and enhance the freshness.

Garnish:
- Before serving, garnish the tropical fruit salad with fresh mint leaves for a burst of freshness.

Serve:
- Serve the Tropical Fruit Salad in bowls or on a platter as a refreshing and colorful side dish or dessert.

Enjoy:
- Enjoy the delightful mix of tropical flavors and the zesty citrus honey dressing in this vibrant fruit salad!

Coconut Prawns

Ingredients:

- 1 pound large prawns, peeled and deveined
- 1 cup shredded coconut
- 1 cup panko breadcrumbs
- 1 cup all-purpose flour
- 2 large eggs, beaten
- Salt and pepper to taste
- Oil for frying

For the Dipping Sauce:

- 1/2 cup sweet chili sauce
- 2 tablespoons soy sauce
- 1 tablespoon lime juice
- 1 tablespoon chopped cilantro

Instructions:

Prepare Prawns:
- Pat the prawns dry with paper towels. Season with salt and pepper.

Set Up Breading Station:
- Set up a breading station with three shallow bowls. Place flour in one, beaten eggs in another, and a mixture of shredded coconut and panko breadcrumbs in the third.

Coat Prawns:
- Dredge each prawn in the flour, shaking off excess. Dip into the beaten eggs, allowing any excess to drip off. Press the prawn into the coconut and breadcrumb mixture, ensuring an even coating. Place on a plate.

Repeat:
- Repeat the process for all prawns, arranging them in a single layer.

Chill (Optional):
- If time allows, you can chill the breaded prawns in the refrigerator for about 15-30 minutes. This helps the coating adhere better during frying.

Heat Oil:
- In a deep fryer or a large, deep skillet, heat oil to 350°F (180°C).

Fry Prawns:

- Carefully lower a few prawns into the hot oil and fry for 2-3 minutes or until golden brown and crispy. Do not overcrowd the pan. Fry in batches if necessary.

Drain:
- Use a slotted spoon to remove the coconut prawns from the oil. Place them on a plate lined with paper towels to drain excess oil.

Prepare Dipping Sauce:
- In a small bowl, mix together sweet chili sauce, soy sauce, lime juice, and chopped cilantro to create the dipping sauce.

Serve:
- Serve the Coconut Prawns hot with the dipping sauce on the side.

Enjoy:
- Enjoy these crispy and flavorful coconut prawns as a delicious appetizer or party snack!

Taro Bubble Tea

Ingredients:

For the Taro Paste:

- 1 cup taro root, peeled and diced
- 1/4 cup sugar
- 1/4 cup coconut milk

For the Bubble Tea:

- 2 tablespoons taro paste (from above)
- 1 cup cooked and chilled black tapioca pearls (boba)
- 1 cup ice cubes
- 1 cup taro-flavored milk (store-bought or homemade)
- 1-2 tablespoons sugar (adjust to taste)

Instructions:

Taro Paste:

Steam Taro:
- Steam the peeled and diced taro root until it becomes soft and easily mashable. This usually takes about 15-20 minutes.

Mash and Sweeten:
- Mash the steamed taro and mix it with sugar and coconut milk while it's still warm. Keep mashing until you achieve a smooth paste. Set aside to cool.

Bubble Tea:

Prepare Tapioca Pearls:
- Cook the black tapioca pearls according to the package instructions. Once cooked, rinse them under cold water and chill them in the refrigerator.

Blend Taro Paste:
- In a blender, combine 2 tablespoons of the taro paste (from the above recipe) with ice cubes, taro-flavored milk, and sugar. Blend until smooth.

Assemble Bubble Tea:

- Place the chilled tapioca pearls at the bottom of a glass. Pour the blended taro mixture over the pearls.

Serve:
- Stir well to combine the tapioca pearls with the taro drink. You can add more ice if desired.

Enjoy:
- Insert a wide straw into the glass, and enjoy sipping on your delicious Taro Bubble Tea!

Note: Adjust the sugar levels and taro paste quantity according to your taste preferences. You can find taro-flavored milk in some grocery stores, or you can make your own by infusing milk with taro flavor.

Pineapple Coconut Smoothie Bowl

Ingredients:

For the Smoothie Bowl:

- 1 cup frozen pineapple chunks
- 1/2 frozen banana
- 1/2 cup coconut milk
- 1/2 cup Greek yogurt (or non-dairy yogurt for a vegan option)
- 1 tablespoon chia seeds (optional)
- 1 tablespoon honey or maple syrup (optional, for sweetness)

For Toppings:

- Fresh pineapple chunks
- Shredded coconut
- Granola
- Sliced banana
- Chia seeds
- Edible flowers (optional)

Instructions:

Blend Smoothie Bowl:
- In a blender, combine frozen pineapple chunks, frozen banana, coconut milk, Greek yogurt, chia seeds (if using), and honey or maple syrup. Blend until smooth and creamy.

Adjust Consistency:
- If the smoothie is too thick, you can add more coconut milk, a little at a time, until you reach your desired consistency.

Pour into Bowl:
- Pour the pineapple coconut smoothie into a bowl.

Add Toppings:
- Arrange fresh pineapple chunks, shredded coconut, granola, sliced banana, chia seeds, and any other desired toppings on top of the smoothie bowl.

Decorate with Edible Flowers (Optional):
- If you have edible flowers, you can use them to add a decorative touch to your smoothie bowl.

Serve Immediately:
- Serve the Pineapple Coconut Smoothie Bowl immediately and enjoy it with a spoon.

Customize:
- Feel free to customize the toppings based on your preferences. You can add nuts, seeds, or other fruits for variation.

Enjoy:
- Enjoy this tropical and refreshing Pineapple Coconut Smoothie Bowl as a nutritious and delicious breakfast or snack!

Hawaiian Bread Pudding

Ingredients:

- 6 cups Hawaiian sweet bread, cut into cubes
- 4 large eggs
- 2 cups whole milk
- 1 cup coconut milk
- 1 cup crushed pineapple, drained
- 1/2 cup brown sugar, packed
- 1/4 cup unsalted butter, melted
- 1 teaspoon vanilla extract
- 1/2 teaspoon ground cinnamon
- 1/4 teaspoon salt
- 1/2 cup shredded coconut (optional, for topping)

For the Coconut Rum Sauce:

- 1/2 cup coconut milk
- 1/4 cup brown sugar, packed
- 2 tablespoons unsalted butter
- 1 tablespoon dark rum (optional)
- 1/4 teaspoon vanilla extract

Instructions:

Preheat Oven:
- Preheat your oven to 350°F (175°C). Grease a baking dish.

Prepare Bread Cubes:
- Cut the Hawaiian sweet bread into cubes and spread them evenly in the greased baking dish.

Prepare Custard Mixture:
- In a large mixing bowl, whisk together the eggs, whole milk, coconut milk, brown sugar, melted butter, vanilla extract, ground cinnamon, and salt until well combined.

Add Pineapple:
- Gently fold in the crushed pineapple into the custard mixture.

Pour Over Bread:

- Pour the custard mixture over the bread cubes, ensuring that all the bread is well-coated. Let it sit for about 15-20 minutes, allowing the bread to absorb the custard.

Bake:
- Bake in the preheated oven for 45-50 minutes or until the top is golden brown, and the pudding is set.

Prepare Coconut Rum Sauce:
- In a small saucepan, combine coconut milk, brown sugar, and butter for the sauce. Cook over medium heat, stirring until the sugar dissolves and the mixture comes to a simmer.

Add Rum and Vanilla:
- If using rum, stir it into the sauce. Remove from heat and add vanilla extract.

Serve:
- Serve the warm Hawaiian Bread Pudding, drizzling the coconut rum sauce over each serving. Optionally, sprinkle shredded coconut on top for added texture.

Enjoy:
- Enjoy this delicious Hawaiian Bread Pudding with a tropical twist!

Mango BBQ Chicken

Ingredients:

- 4 boneless, skinless chicken breasts
- Salt and pepper to taste
- 1 cup mango puree
- 1/2 cup barbecue sauce
- 2 tablespoons soy sauce
- 2 tablespoons honey
- 2 cloves garlic, minced
- 1 teaspoon ground ginger
- 1/2 teaspoon smoked paprika
- 1/4 teaspoon cayenne pepper (optional, for heat)
- Fresh cilantro, chopped, for garnish

Instructions:

Preheat Grill:
- Preheat your grill to medium-high heat.

Season Chicken:
- Season the chicken breasts with salt and pepper to taste.

Prepare Mango BBQ Sauce:
- In a blender, combine mango puree, barbecue sauce, soy sauce, honey, minced garlic, ground ginger, smoked paprika, and cayenne pepper (if using). Blend until smooth.

Set Aside Some Sauce:
- Set aside a portion of the mango BBQ sauce for basting and serving later.

Grill Chicken:
- Place the seasoned chicken breasts on the preheated grill. Grill for about 5-7 minutes per side or until the internal temperature reaches 165°F (74°C) and the chicken is cooked through.

Baste with Sauce:
- During the last few minutes of grilling, baste the chicken with the mango BBQ sauce. Ensure both sides are well-coated.

Rest and Garnish:
- Remove the chicken from the grill and let it rest for a few minutes. Garnish with freshly chopped cilantro.

Serve:
- Serve the Mango BBQ Chicken with the reserved mango BBQ sauce on the side for dipping or drizzling.

Enjoy:
- Enjoy this tropical twist on BBQ chicken with the sweet and savory flavors of mango!

Tuna Poke Bowl

Ingredients:

For the Poke:

- 1 pound sushi-grade tuna, diced
- 1/4 cup soy sauce
- 1 tablespoon sesame oil
- 1 tablespoon rice vinegar
- 1 teaspoon honey
- 1 teaspoon ginger, grated
- 1 teaspoon garlic, minced
- 1 tablespoon green onions, finely chopped
- 1 teaspoon sesame seeds
- Red pepper flakes to taste (optional)

For the Bowl:

- 2 cups cooked sushi rice, cooled
- 1 cup edamame, shelled
- 1 avocado, sliced
- 1 cucumber, sliced
- 1 carrot, julienned
- 1 radish, thinly sliced
- Nori strips (seaweed), for garnish
- Pickled ginger and wasabi, for serving

Instructions:

Prepare Poke Marinade:
- In a bowl, whisk together soy sauce, sesame oil, rice vinegar, honey, grated ginger, minced garlic, chopped green onions, sesame seeds, and red pepper flakes (if using).

Dice Tuna:
- Cut the sushi-grade tuna into bite-sized cubes.

Marinate Tuna:

- Gently toss the diced tuna in the prepared poke marinade until well coated. Refrigerate for at least 15-30 minutes to let the flavors meld.

Assemble Poke Bowl:
- In serving bowls, arrange a bed of cooked sushi rice.

Add Toppings:
- Top the rice with marinated tuna, sliced avocado, cucumber, julienned carrot, radish slices, and shelled edamame.

Garnish:
- Garnish the poke bowl with nori strips for added flavor and texture.

Serve:
- Serve the Tuna Poke Bowl with pickled ginger and wasabi on the side.

Enjoy:
- Enjoy this refreshing and flavorful Tuna Poke Bowl, a delicious and healthy dish inspired by Hawaiian cuisine!

Pineapple Upside-Down Cake

Ingredients:

For the Topping:

- 1/2 cup unsalted butter
- 1 cup brown sugar, packed
- 1 can pineapple slices, drained
- Maraschino cherries, for decoration

For the Cake Batter:

- 1 and 1/2 cups all-purpose flour
- 1 and 1/2 teaspoons baking powder
- 1/2 teaspoon salt
- 1/2 cup unsalted butter, softened
- 1 cup granulated sugar
- 2 large eggs
- 1 teaspoon vanilla extract
- 3/4 cup buttermilk

Instructions:

Preheat Oven:
- Preheat your oven to 350°F (175°C).

Prepare Topping:
- Melt 1/2 cup of unsalted butter and pour it into a 9-inch round cake pan. Sprinkle the brown sugar evenly over the melted butter.

Arrange Pineapple Slices:
- Arrange the pineapple slices on top of the brown sugar in a decorative pattern. Place a maraschino cherry in the center of each pineapple slice and in any gaps.

Prepare Cake Batter:
- In a medium bowl, whisk together the flour, baking powder, and salt.

Cream Butter and Sugar:
- In a separate large bowl, cream together 1/2 cup softened butter and granulated sugar until light and fluffy.

Add Eggs and Vanilla:

- Beat in the eggs one at a time, then stir in the vanilla extract.

Alternate Mixing:
- Gradually add the dry ingredients to the butter and sugar mixture, alternating with buttermilk. Begin and end with the dry ingredients. Mix until just combined.

Pour Batter Over Pineapples:
- Pour the cake batter over the arranged pineapple slices in the cake pan, spreading it evenly.

Bake:
- Bake in the preheated oven for 40-45 minutes or until a toothpick inserted into the center comes out clean.

Cool and Invert:
- Allow the cake to cool for about 10 minutes in the pan. Then, invert the cake onto a serving plate.

Serve:
- Serve the Pineapple Upside-Down Cake warm or at room temperature.

Enjoy:
- Enjoy this classic and delicious Pineapple Upside-Down Cake with its caramelized pineapple and cherry topping!

Kalbi Short Ribs

Ingredients:

- 3 pounds beef short ribs, cut flanken-style (across the bone)
- 1 cup soy sauce
- 1/2 cup brown sugar
- 1/4 cup mirin (Japanese sweet rice wine)
- 1/4 cup rice vinegar
- 3 tablespoons sesame oil
- 4 cloves garlic, minced
- 1 tablespoon fresh ginger, grated
- 2 green onions, finely chopped (for garnish)
- Toasted sesame seeds (for garnish)

Instructions:

Marinate the Short Ribs:
- In a bowl, whisk together soy sauce, brown sugar, mirin, rice vinegar, sesame oil, minced garlic, and grated ginger to make the marinade.

Prepare Short Ribs:
- Place the beef short ribs in a large resealable plastic bag or a shallow dish.

Marinate:
- Pour the marinade over the short ribs, ensuring they are well coated. Seal the bag or cover the dish, and marinate in the refrigerator for at least 4 hours or overnight for best results.

Preheat Grill:
- Preheat your grill to medium-high heat.

Grill Short Ribs:
- Remove the short ribs from the marinade and shake off excess liquid. Grill the ribs for about 5-7 minutes per side or until they are nicely browned and cooked to your preferred doneness.

Baste with Marinade:
- While grilling, you can baste the short ribs with some of the marinade for added flavor.

Garnish:

- Once done, remove the short ribs from the grill and place them on a serving platter. Garnish with chopped green onions and toasted sesame seeds.

Serve:
- Serve the Kalbi Short Ribs hot with your favorite side dishes, such as steamed rice or kimchi.

Enjoy:
- Enjoy the delicious flavors of Korean-style Kalbi Short Ribs, perfect for a barbecue or grilling occasion!

Hawaiian Acai Bowl

Ingredients:

For the Acai Bowl Base:

- 2 frozen Acai berry packets
- 1/2 cup frozen mixed berries (strawberries, blueberries, raspberries)
- 1 ripe banana, frozen
- 1/2 cup coconut water or almond milk
- 1 tablespoon honey or agave syrup (optional, for sweetness)

For Toppings:

- Sliced banana
- Fresh berries (blueberries, strawberries, raspberries)
- Granola
- Shredded coconut
- Chia seeds
- Sliced almonds
- Honey or agave syrup for drizzling

Instructions:

Prepare Acai Packets:
- Run the frozen Acai berry packets under warm water for a few seconds to slightly thaw them. Break the packets into chunks.

Blend Acai Base:
- In a blender, combine the Acai berry chunks, frozen mixed berries, frozen banana, coconut water (or almond milk), and honey or agave syrup (if using). Blend until smooth and creamy.

Adjust Consistency:
- If the mixture is too thick, you can add more coconut water or almond milk, a little at a time, until you reach your desired consistency.

Pour into Bowl:
- Pour the Acai mixture into a bowl.

Add Toppings:

- Arrange sliced banana, fresh berries, granola, shredded coconut, chia seeds, sliced almonds, and any other desired toppings on top of the Acai bowl.

Drizzle with Honey:

- Drizzle honey or agave syrup over the toppings for extra sweetness.

Serve Immediately:

- Serve the Hawaiian Acai Bowl immediately and enjoy it with a spoon.

Customize:

- Feel free to customize the toppings based on your preferences. You can add nuts, seeds, or other fruits for variation.

Enjoy:

- Enjoy this refreshing and nutritious Hawaiian Acai Bowl as a wholesome breakfast or snack!

Coconut Crusted Fish Tacos

Ingredients:

For the Coconut Crusted Fish:

- 1 pound white fish fillets (such as cod or tilapia)
- 1 cup shredded coconut
- 1/2 cup breadcrumbs
- 1/2 cup all-purpose flour
- 2 teaspoons cumin
- 1 teaspoon garlic powder
- 1/2 teaspoon salt
- 1/4 teaspoon black pepper
- 2 large eggs, beaten
- Cooking oil for frying

For the Cabbage Slaw:

- 2 cups shredded green cabbage
- 1/4 cup chopped fresh cilantro
- 1/4 cup mayonnaise
- 1 tablespoon lime juice
- Salt and pepper to taste

For Assembling Tacos:

- Flour or corn tortillas
- Sliced avocado
- Lime wedges
- Salsa or hot sauce (optional)

Instructions:

Prepare Coconut Crusted Fish:
- In a bowl, combine shredded coconut, breadcrumbs, all-purpose flour, cumin, garlic powder, salt, and black pepper. Mix well.

Coat Fish Fillets:
- Dip each fish fillet into the beaten eggs, ensuring it is fully coated. Then, dredge the fish in the coconut mixture, pressing gently to adhere the coating.

Fry the Fish:
- In a large skillet, heat cooking oil over medium-high heat. Fry the coated fish fillets for 3-4 minutes per side or until the crust is golden brown and the fish is cooked through. Place the cooked fillets on a paper towel-lined plate to drain excess oil.

Prepare Cabbage Slaw:
- In a bowl, combine shredded green cabbage, chopped cilantro, mayonnaise, lime juice, salt, and pepper. Toss until well combined.

Warm Tortillas:
- Warm the tortillas in a dry skillet or microwave.

Assemble Tacos:
- Place a spoonful of the cabbage slaw on each tortilla. Top with a coconut-crusted fish fillet. Add sliced avocado on top.

Garnish:
- Garnish with additional cilantro, lime wedges, and salsa or hot sauce if desired.

Serve Immediately:
- Serve the Coconut Crusted Fish Tacos immediately and enjoy this delicious and tropical twist on fish tacos!

Mango Habanero Chicken Wings

Ingredients:

For the Chicken Wings:

- 2 pounds chicken wings, split at joints, tips discarded
- 1 tablespoon olive oil
- Salt and pepper to taste
- 1 teaspoon garlic powder
- 1 teaspoon onion powder
- 1 teaspoon smoked paprika
- 1/2 teaspoon cayenne pepper (optional, for heat)

For the Mango Habanero Sauce:

- 1 cup mango puree
- 2 habanero peppers, seeds removed and finely chopped
- 1/4 cup honey
- 2 tablespoons soy sauce
- 2 tablespoons apple cider vinegar
- 1 teaspoon garlic, minced
- 1 teaspoon ginger, grated
- Salt to taste
- Fresh cilantro, chopped (for garnish)

Instructions:

Preheat Oven:
- Preheat your oven to 400°F (200°C).

Prepare Chicken Wings:
- In a large bowl, toss the chicken wings with olive oil, salt, pepper, garlic powder, onion powder, smoked paprika, and cayenne pepper (if using).

Bake Chicken Wings:
- Place the seasoned chicken wings on a baking sheet lined with parchment paper. Bake in the preheated oven for 40-45 minutes or until the wings are crispy and cooked through, flipping them halfway through.

Prepare Mango Habanero Sauce:
- In a saucepan over medium heat, combine mango puree, chopped habanero peppers, honey, soy sauce, apple cider vinegar, minced garlic, and grated ginger. Bring the mixture to a simmer, stirring frequently.

Simmer and Season:
- Reduce the heat and let the sauce simmer for about 10-15 minutes or until it thickens slightly. Season with salt to taste.

Coat Wings in Sauce:
- Once the chicken wings are done baking, transfer them to a large bowl. Pour the mango habanero sauce over the wings and toss until they are well coated in the sauce.

Garnish:
- Garnish the wings with chopped fresh cilantro.

Serve:
- Serve the Mango Habanero Chicken Wings hot, and enjoy the sweet and spicy flavors!

Optional Grilling:
- If you prefer, you can also grill the seasoned chicken wings and then toss them in the mango habanero sauce for a smoky flavor.

Hawaiian Sweet Rolls

Ingredients:

- 4 cups all-purpose flour
- 1/2 cup granulated sugar
- 1 packet (2 1/4 teaspoons) active dry yeast
- 1 teaspoon salt
- 1/2 cup unsalted butter, melted
- 3/4 cup pineapple juice, lukewarm
- 1/4 cup whole milk, lukewarm
- 2 large eggs

Instructions:

Activate Yeast:
- In a bowl, combine lukewarm pineapple juice and milk. Sprinkle the yeast over the liquid, add a pinch of sugar, and let it sit for about 5-10 minutes until frothy.

Mix Dry Ingredients:
- In a large bowl, whisk together flour, sugar, and salt.

Combine Wet Ingredients:
- In another bowl, whisk together the melted butter and eggs.

Make Dough:
- Pour the activated yeast mixture into the flour mixture, followed by the melted butter and egg mixture. Mix until a dough forms.

Knead Dough:
- Turn the dough onto a floured surface and knead for about 8-10 minutes or until it becomes smooth and elastic.

First Rise:
- Place the dough in a greased bowl, cover it with a clean kitchen towel, and let it rise in a warm place for about 1-1.5 hours or until it doubles in size.

Punch Down and Shape:
- Punch down the dough and turn it out onto a floured surface. Divide it into equal portions and shape them into rolls.

Second Rise:
- Place the shaped rolls on a baking sheet lined with parchment paper. Cover them with a towel and let them rise for another 30-45 minutes.

Preheat Oven:
- Preheat your oven to 350°F (175°C).

Bake:
- Bake the rolls in the preheated oven for 15-20 minutes or until they turn golden brown.

Cool:
- Allow the Hawaiian Sweet Rolls to cool on a wire rack before serving.

Enjoy:
- Serve these delightful Hawaiian Sweet Rolls warm or at room temperature, and enjoy their soft, slightly sweet flavor!

Pineapple Coconut Rice

Ingredients:

- 1 cup long-grain white rice
- 1 cup coconut milk
- 1 cup water
- 1 cup fresh pineapple, diced
- 1 tablespoon coconut oil
- 1/2 teaspoon salt
- 1/4 cup shredded coconut (optional, for garnish)
- Fresh cilantro, chopped (optional, for garnish)

Instructions:

Rinse Rice:
- Rinse the rice under cold water until the water runs clear to remove excess starch.

Combine Ingredients:
- In a saucepan, combine the rinsed rice, coconut milk, water, coconut oil, and salt.

Bring to a Boil:
- Bring the mixture to a boil over medium-high heat.

Simmer:
- Reduce the heat to low, cover the saucepan with a tight-fitting lid, and let it simmer for 18-20 minutes or until the rice is tender and has absorbed the liquid.

Add Pineapple:
- Gently fold in the diced pineapple into the cooked rice. Cover the saucepan and let it sit for an additional 5 minutes to allow the flavors to meld.

Fluff Rice:
- Fluff the rice with a fork to separate the grains.

Garnish:
- If desired, garnish the Pineapple Coconut Rice with shredded coconut and chopped fresh cilantro.

Serve:
- Serve the Pineapple Coconut Rice as a side dish to complement various Asian and tropical-inspired main courses.

Enjoy:
- Enjoy the sweet and savory flavors of this Pineapple Coconut Rice as a delightful accompaniment to your favorite dishes!

Hawaiian Seafood Paella

Ingredients:

- 1 cup Arborio rice
- 1/2 pound large shrimp, peeled and deveined
- 1/2 pound mussels, cleaned and debearded
- 1/2 pound clams, scrubbed
- 1/2 pound squid, cleaned and sliced into rings
- 1/2 cup diced pineapple
- 1/2 cup diced bell peppers (red and yellow)
- 1/2 cup diced tomatoes
- 1/4 cup frozen peas
- 1/4 cup chopped cilantro
- 1 onion, finely chopped
- 3 cloves garlic, minced
- 1 teaspoon smoked paprika
- 1 teaspoon saffron threads
- 1/2 teaspoon turmeric
- 4 cups seafood or chicken broth
- 1/4 cup dry white wine
- 2 tablespoons olive oil
- Salt and pepper to taste
- Lemon wedges for serving

Instructions:

Prepare Saffron Broth:
- In a small bowl, steep the saffron threads in warm water or broth for about 10-15 minutes to infuse the color and flavor.

Preheat Oven:
- Preheat your oven to 375°F (190°C).

Season Seafood:
- Season the shrimp, mussels, clams, and squid with salt, pepper, and smoked paprika.

Sear Seafood:

- In a large oven-safe paella pan or skillet, heat olive oil over medium-high heat. Sear the shrimp, mussels, clams, and squid until they are lightly browned. Remove them from the pan and set aside.

Sauté Aromatics:
- In the same pan, sauté the chopped onion and garlic until they become translucent.

Add Rice and Vegetables:
- Stir in the Arborio rice and cook for 2-3 minutes until it's well-coated with the aromatics. Add diced pineapple, bell peppers, tomatoes, peas, and chopped cilantro. Mix well.

Add Saffron Broth:
- Pour in the saffron-infused broth, dry white wine, and seafood or chicken broth. Bring the mixture to a gentle boil.

Bake in the Oven:
- Transfer the paella pan to the preheated oven and bake for 20-25 minutes or until the rice is cooked and has absorbed the liquid.

Add Seared Seafood:
- Carefully place the seared seafood on top of the rice.

Continue Baking:
- Return the pan to the oven and bake for an additional 10-15 minutes or until the seafood is fully cooked and the edges of the rice are crispy.

Serve:
- Remove the Hawaiian Seafood Paella from the oven, let it rest for a few minutes, and then serve it with lemon wedges.

Enjoy:
- Enjoy this flavorful Hawaiian twist on classic paella with a delightful combination of seafood and tropical ingredients!

Macadamia Nut Crusted Mahi Mahi

Ingredients:

- 4 Mahi Mahi fillets
- 1 cup macadamia nuts, finely chopped
- 1/2 cup Panko breadcrumbs
- 1/4 cup flour
- 2 eggs, beaten
- 2 tablespoons Dijon mustard
- 2 tablespoons honey
- 1 teaspoon garlic powder
- 1 teaspoon onion powder
- Salt and pepper to taste
- 2 tablespoons olive oil
- Lemon wedges for serving
- Fresh parsley, chopped (for garnish)

Instructions:

Preheat Oven:
- Preheat your oven to 400°F (200°C).

Prepare Crust Mixture:
- In a shallow dish, combine finely chopped macadamia nuts, Panko breadcrumbs, garlic powder, onion powder, salt, and pepper.

Dredge Mahi Mahi:
- Dredge each Mahi Mahi fillet in flour, shaking off excess. Then, dip them into the beaten eggs, and finally coat them with the macadamia nut mixture, pressing the nuts onto the fish to adhere.

Prepare Honey Mustard Glaze:
- In a small bowl, whisk together Dijon mustard and honey.

Sear Mahi Mahi:
- Heat olive oil in an oven-safe skillet over medium-high heat. Sear the Mahi Mahi fillets for 2-3 minutes per side until the crust is golden brown.

Apply Honey Mustard Glaze:
- Brush the tops of the fillets with the honey mustard glaze.

Bake in the Oven:

- Transfer the skillet to the preheated oven and bake for 10-12 minutes or until the Mahi Mahi is cooked through and flakes easily with a fork.

Garnish:
- Garnish with chopped fresh parsley and serve the Macadamia Nut Crusted Mahi Mahi hot.

Serve with Lemon Wedges:
- Serve with lemon wedges on the side for an extra burst of freshness.

Enjoy:
- Enjoy this delicious Macadamia Nut Crusted Mahi Mahi as a delightful and nutty twist on a classic seafood dish!

Mango Sticky Rice

Ingredients:

For Sticky Rice:

- 1 cup glutinous rice (also known as sweet rice)
- 1 cup coconut milk
- 1/2 cup sugar
- 1/2 teaspoon salt

For Mango Topping:

- 2 ripe mangoes, peeled, pitted, and sliced
- Sesame seeds (optional, for garnish)
- Coconut flakes (optional, for garnish)

Instructions:

Soak Sticky Rice:
- Rinse the glutinous rice under cold water until the water runs clear. Soak the rice in water for at least 4 hours or preferably overnight.

Steam Sticky Rice:
- Drain the soaked rice. Place the rice in a steamer lined with cheesecloth or a clean kitchen towel. Steam the rice for 25-30 minutes or until it becomes tender.

Prepare Coconut Sauce:
- While the rice is steaming, in a saucepan, combine coconut milk, sugar, and salt. Heat the mixture over medium heat, stirring until the sugar dissolves. Remove from heat and set aside.

Mix Sticky Rice with Coconut Sauce:
- Once the sticky rice is cooked, transfer it to a bowl. Pour half of the coconut sauce over the rice and gently fold until well combined. Let it sit for a few minutes to allow the rice to absorb the flavors.

Serve Sticky Rice:
- Spoon the sweetened sticky rice onto serving plates.

Slice Mangoes:

- Slice the ripe mangoes into thin strips.

Arrange Mango Topping:
- Arrange the sliced mangoes on top of the sticky rice.

Drizzle with Coconut Sauce:
- Drizzle the remaining coconut sauce over the mangoes and sticky rice.

Garnish:
- Optionally, garnish with sesame seeds and coconut flakes for added texture and flavor.

Serve Warm:
- Serve the Mango Sticky Rice warm and enjoy the delightful combination of sweet, sticky rice with creamy coconut sauce and fresh mango slices.

Teriyaki Glazed Salmon

Ingredients:

- 4 salmon fillets
- 1/4 cup soy sauce
- 2 tablespoons sake or white wine
- 2 tablespoons mirin
- 2 tablespoons honey
- 1 tablespoon brown sugar
- 1 tablespoon fresh ginger, grated
- 2 cloves garlic, minced
- 1 tablespoon vegetable oil (for cooking)
- Sesame seeds and green onions for garnish (optional)

Instructions:

Prepare Teriyaki Sauce:
- In a small bowl, whisk together soy sauce, sake (or white wine), mirin, honey, brown sugar, grated ginger, and minced garlic to create the teriyaki sauce.

Marinate Salmon:
- Place the salmon fillets in a shallow dish or a resealable plastic bag. Pour half of the teriyaki sauce over the salmon, ensuring each fillet is coated. Allow the salmon to marinate for at least 15-30 minutes in the refrigerator.

Reserve Sauce:
- Reserve the remaining teriyaki sauce for later use.

Preheat Oven:
- Preheat your oven to 400°F (200°C).

Cook Salmon:
- Heat vegetable oil in an oven-safe skillet over medium-high heat. Remove the salmon from the marinade and place it skin-side down in the skillet. Sear for 2-3 minutes until the skin is golden brown.

Brush with Sauce:
- Brush the top of each salmon fillet with some of the reserved teriyaki sauce.

Bake in the Oven:

- Transfer the skillet to the preheated oven and bake for 8-10 minutes or until the salmon is cooked to your liking.

Glaze with More Sauce:
- During the last few minutes of baking, brush the salmon with more teriyaki sauce to create a glossy glaze.

Garnish:
- Optionally, garnish the Teriyaki Glazed Salmon with sesame seeds and chopped green onions.

Serve:
- Serve the salmon hot over rice or with your favorite side dishes.

Enjoy:
- Enjoy the flavorful and succulent Teriyaki Glazed Salmon with a perfect balance of sweet and savory notes!

Hawaiian Chicken Katsu

Ingredients:

For Chicken:

- 4 boneless, skinless chicken breasts
- Salt and pepper to taste
- 1 cup all-purpose flour
- 2 large eggs, beaten
- 2 cups Panko breadcrumbs
- Vegetable oil for frying

For Tonkatsu Sauce:

- 1/2 cup ketchup
- 3 tablespoons Worcestershire sauce
- 2 tablespoons soy sauce
- 2 tablespoons mirin (or rice vinegar)
- 2 tablespoons sugar
- 1 teaspoon Dijon mustard

For Serving:

- Cooked white rice
- Shredded cabbage (optional)
- Lemon wedges (optional)

Instructions:

Prep Chicken:
- Season the chicken breasts with salt and pepper.

Coat in Flour:
- Dredge each chicken breast in flour, shaking off any excess.

Dip in Egg:
- Dip the floured chicken breasts into the beaten eggs.

Coat in Panko:

- Press each chicken breast into the Panko breadcrumbs, ensuring an even coating.

Chill:
- Place the breaded chicken breasts in the refrigerator for about 15-20 minutes. This helps the coating adhere better during frying.

Prepare Tonkatsu Sauce:
- In a small saucepan, combine ketchup, Worcestershire sauce, soy sauce, mirin, sugar, and Dijon mustard. Heat over low heat, stirring, until the sugar dissolves. Simmer for a few minutes until the sauce thickens slightly. Set aside.

Heat Oil:
- In a large skillet, heat vegetable oil over medium-high heat for frying.

Fry Chicken:
- Fry the breaded chicken breasts for 4-5 minutes per side or until golden brown and cooked through. Ensure the internal temperature reaches 165°F (74°C).

Drain on Paper Towels:
- Transfer the fried chicken to a plate lined with paper towels to drain any excess oil.

Slice Chicken:
- Let the chicken rest for a few minutes, then slice it into strips.

Serve:
- Serve the Hawaiian Chicken Katsu over cooked white rice. Optionally, serve with shredded cabbage on the side and lemon wedges.

Drizzle with Tonkatsu Sauce:
- Drizzle the Tonkatsu sauce over the chicken or serve it on the side for dipping.

Enjoy:
- Enjoy this Hawaiian twist on Chicken Katsu, combining crispy breaded chicken with a flavorful Tonkatsu sauce!

Pineapple Coleslaw

Ingredients:

- 4 cups shredded green cabbage
- 1 cup shredded carrots
- 1 cup fresh pineapple, finely chopped
- 1/2 cup mayonnaise
- 1/4 cup Greek yogurt or sour cream
- 2 tablespoons apple cider vinegar
- 2 tablespoons honey
- Salt and pepper to taste
- 1/4 cup chopped fresh cilantro (optional, for garnish)

Instructions:

Prepare Vegetables:
- In a large bowl, combine shredded green cabbage and shredded carrots.

Add Pineapple:
- Add finely chopped fresh pineapple to the bowl with the shredded vegetables.

Make Dressing:
- In a separate bowl, whisk together mayonnaise, Greek yogurt or sour cream, apple cider vinegar, honey, salt, and pepper. Adjust the sweetness and acidity to your taste.

Combine:
- Pour the dressing over the cabbage, carrots, and pineapple. Toss everything together until the coleslaw is well coated in the dressing.

Chill:
- Cover the bowl and refrigerate the Pineapple Coleslaw for at least 30 minutes to allow the flavors to meld and the coleslaw to chill.

Garnish:
- Before serving, if desired, garnish with chopped fresh cilantro for a burst of herbaceous flavor.

Serve:
- Serve the Pineapple Coleslaw as a refreshing and tropical side dish with grilled meats, fish, or as a topping for sandwiches and tacos.

Enjoy:

- Enjoy the sweet and tangy goodness of this Pineapple Coleslaw that adds a tropical twist to your meal!

Tropical Fruit Popsicles

Ingredients:

- 2 cups pineapple chunks
- 1 cup mango chunks
- 1 cup kiwi slices
- 1 cup strawberries, hulled and halved
- 1 cup coconut water or coconut milk
- 1-2 tablespoons honey or agave syrup (optional, based on sweetness preference)
- Popsicle molds and sticks

Instructions:

Prepare Fruits:
- Prepare the fruits by cutting them into bite-sized pieces.

Layer the Molds:
- Begin by layering the popsicle molds with a variety of tropical fruits. You can create different layers for a visually appealing popsicle.

Mix Coconut Liquid:
- In a blender, combine coconut water or coconut milk with honey or agave syrup. Blend until smooth.

Fill Molds:
- Pour the coconut mixture into the popsicle molds over the layered fruits. Leave a little space at the top to allow for expansion.

Insert Sticks:
- Place the sticks into the molds, ensuring they are centered in each popsicle.

Freeze:
- Freeze the popsicles for at least 4-6 hours or until fully set.

Unmold Popsicles:
- Once the popsicles are frozen, run the molds briefly under warm water to help release the popsicles.

Serve:
- Serve these refreshing Tropical Fruit Popsicles on a hot day for a cool and fruity treat.

Enjoy:

- Enjoy the burst of tropical flavors with every bite of these homemade popsicles!

Grilled Tofu with Pineapple Salsa

Ingredients:

For Grilled Tofu:

- 1 block firm tofu, pressed and sliced into rectangles
- 2 tablespoons soy sauce
- 1 tablespoon olive oil
- 1 tablespoon maple syrup or agave nectar
- 1 teaspoon smoked paprika
- 1 teaspoon garlic powder
- Salt and pepper to taste

For Pineapple Salsa:

- 1 cup fresh pineapple, diced
- 1/2 cup red bell pepper, diced
- 1/4 cup red onion, finely chopped
- 1/4 cup fresh cilantro, chopped
- 1 jalapeño, seeds removed and finely chopped (optional for heat)
- Juice of 1 lime
- Salt to taste

Instructions:

Marinate Tofu:
- In a bowl, whisk together soy sauce, olive oil, maple syrup or agave nectar, smoked paprika, garlic powder, salt, and pepper. Place the tofu slices in a shallow dish and pour the marinade over them. Allow the tofu to marinate for at least 30 minutes.

Preheat Grill:
- Preheat your grill or grill pan over medium-high heat.

Grill Tofu:
- Grill the marinated tofu slices for about 4-5 minutes on each side or until grill marks form, and the tofu is heated through.

Prepare Pineapple Salsa:

- In a bowl, combine diced pineapple, red bell pepper, red onion, cilantro, jalapeño (if using), lime juice, and a pinch of salt. Mix well.

Serve:
- Place the grilled tofu on a serving platter and top it with the refreshing pineapple salsa.

Garnish:
- Optionally, garnish with additional cilantro or lime wedges.

Enjoy:
- Enjoy this Grilled Tofu with Pineapple Salsa as a flavorful, plant-based dish that combines smoky grilled tofu with the sweetness and tanginess of the pineapple salsa!

Hawaiian Lemonade

Ingredients:

- 1 cup freshly squeezed lemon juice (about 4-6 lemons)
- 1/2 cup pineapple juice
- 1/4 cup honey or agave syrup (adjust to taste)
- 4 cups cold water
- Ice cubes
- Lemon slices and pineapple wedges for garnish
- Mint leaves for garnish (optional)

Instructions:

Prepare Lemon Juice:
- Squeeze lemons to obtain 1 cup of fresh lemon juice. Remove any seeds.

Mix Sweetener:
- In a pitcher, combine the freshly squeezed lemon juice with pineapple juice and honey or agave syrup. Stir well until the sweetener is completely dissolved.

Add Cold Water:
- Pour cold water into the pitcher and mix until all the ingredients are well combined.

Taste and Adjust:
- Taste the lemonade and adjust the sweetness by adding more honey or agave syrup if needed.

Chill:
- Place the pitcher in the refrigerator to chill the lemonade.

Serve over Ice:
- Fill glasses with ice cubes and pour the Hawaiian Lemonade over the ice.

Garnish:
- Garnish the glasses with lemon slices, pineapple wedges, and mint leaves if desired.

Stir Before Serving:
- Give the lemonade a gentle stir before serving to ensure that the flavors are well-mixed.

Enjoy:

- Enjoy the refreshing taste of Hawaiian Lemonade on a hot day or as a tropical beverage for any occasion!

Mango Coconut Sorbet

Ingredients:

- 3 cups ripe mango chunks (about 3 medium-sized mangoes)
- 1 can (13.5 oz) coconut milk
- 1/2 cup granulated sugar (adjust to taste)
- 1 tablespoon lime juice
- Pinch of salt

Instructions:

Prepare Mango:
- Peel and dice the ripe mangoes, discarding the pit.

Blend Ingredients:
- In a blender, combine the mango chunks, coconut milk, granulated sugar, lime juice, and a pinch of salt. Blend until smooth and creamy.

Taste and Adjust:
- Taste the mixture and adjust the sweetness by adding more sugar if needed. Blend again to incorporate any additional sugar.

Chill Mixture:
- Pour the mango coconut mixture into a bowl or container. Cover and refrigerate for at least 2 hours to chill the mixture.

Churn in Ice Cream Maker (Optional):
- If you have an ice cream maker, churn the chilled mixture according to the manufacturer's instructions until it reaches a sorbet-like consistency.

Freeze Without Ice Cream Maker:
- If you don't have an ice cream maker, simply transfer the chilled mixture to a lidded container and place it in the freezer. Every 30 minutes, stir the mixture with a fork to break up ice crystals, repeating this process for about 3-4 hours or until the sorbet is firm.

Serve:
- Once the Mango Coconut Sorbet reaches the desired consistency, scoop it into bowls or cones.

Garnish (Optional):
- Garnish with fresh mango slices, mint leaves, or a sprinkle of shredded coconut.

Enjoy:

- Enjoy this luscious and tropical Mango Coconut Sorbet as a delightful frozen treat!

Hawaiian Sweet Potato Salad

Ingredients:

- 3 large sweet potatoes, peeled and cubed
- 1 cup fresh pineapple, diced
- 1/2 cup red onion, finely chopped
- 1/4 cup fresh cilantro, chopped
- 1/4 cup macadamia nuts, chopped
- 1/4 cup mayonnaise
- 2 tablespoons Greek yogurt or sour cream
- 1 tablespoon Dijon mustard
- 1 tablespoon honey
- Salt and pepper to taste

Instructions:

Cook Sweet Potatoes:
- Boil or steam the sweet potato cubes until they are fork-tender. Drain and let them cool to room temperature.

Prepare Pineapple:
- Dice the fresh pineapple into small, bite-sized pieces.

Make Dressing:
- In a small bowl, whisk together mayonnaise, Greek yogurt or sour cream, Dijon mustard, honey, salt, and pepper. Adjust the sweetness and seasoning to your liking.

Combine Ingredients:
- In a large mixing bowl, combine the cooked sweet potatoes, diced pineapple, finely chopped red onion, chopped cilantro, and macadamia nuts.

Add Dressing:
- Pour the prepared dressing over the sweet potato mixture. Gently toss until all ingredients are well coated in the dressing.

Chill:
- Cover the bowl and refrigerate the Hawaiian Sweet Potato Salad for at least 1-2 hours to allow the flavors to meld.

Serve:

- Once chilled, give the salad a final gentle toss and serve it in a bowl or on a platter.

Garnish (Optional):
- Garnish with additional chopped cilantro or macadamia nuts if desired.

Enjoy:
- Enjoy this unique and flavorful Hawaiian Sweet Potato Salad as a side dish at your next barbecue or as a refreshing addition to any meal!

Coconut Pineapple Bread

Ingredients:

- 2 cups all-purpose flour
- 1 teaspoon baking powder
- 1/2 teaspoon baking soda
- 1/2 teaspoon salt
- 1 cup shredded coconut (sweetened or unsweetened)
- 1 cup crushed pineapple, drained
- 1/2 cup unsalted butter, softened
- 1 cup granulated sugar
- 2 large eggs
- 1 teaspoon vanilla extract
- 1 cup coconut milk

Instructions:

Preheat Oven:
- Preheat your oven to 350°F (175°C). Grease and flour a 9x5-inch loaf pan.

Mix Dry Ingredients:
- In a medium bowl, whisk together the all-purpose flour, baking powder, baking soda, and salt. Stir in the shredded coconut.

Prepare Pineapple:
- Drain the crushed pineapple to remove excess liquid.

Cream Butter and Sugar:
- In a large mixing bowl, cream together the softened butter and granulated sugar until light and fluffy.

Add Eggs and Vanilla:
- Add the eggs one at a time, beating well after each addition. Stir in the vanilla extract.

Alternate Wet and Dry Ingredients:
- Gradually add the dry ingredients to the wet ingredients, alternating with the coconut milk. Begin and end with the dry ingredients. Mix until just combined.

Fold in Pineapple:
- Gently fold in the drained crushed pineapple until evenly distributed in the batter.

Transfer to Pan:

- Pour the batter into the prepared loaf pan, spreading it evenly.

Bake:
- Bake in the preheated oven for approximately 50-60 minutes or until a toothpick inserted into the center comes out clean.

Cool:
- Allow the Coconut Pineapple Bread to cool in the pan for 10-15 minutes, then transfer it to a wire rack to cool completely.

Slice and Serve:
- Once cooled, slice the bread and serve. It's delicious on its own or with a spread of butter.

Enjoy:
- Enjoy this tropical-flavored Coconut Pineapple Bread as a delightful treat for breakfast or snack time!